"Geof Jowett is a healer, mystic, and altogether a wonderful spiritual teacher. Science and Spirit mix beautifully with him."
—**JAMES VAN PRAAGH**, author of the #1 New York Times bestseller Talking to Heaven

"The Power of I AM is the perfect guidebook for anyone interested in higher consciousness and truth. Geoffrey Jowett has a profound understanding of how to integrate the powerful forces of the chakra system into everyday life, and he teaches us how to maintain meaningful awareness through the alignment of our energy systems."
—**MICHELLE CROMER**, author of Exit Strategy: Thinking Outside the Box

"While I could have read Geoffrey Jowett's gem of a book, The Power of I AM, in one sitting, I savored it and read it a little at a time over a few weeks. I find it to be like a 'book of hours' in the classic sense. I used it as a springboard for meditation and urge you to keep it close at hand."
—**L. D. THOMPSON**, author of The Message and Fields of Plenty

"The Power of I AM inspires our education and exploration of our True Self. This precious creation belongs in your purse, by the bed, in your yoga class . . . or give it as a gift. The eclectic overlay is inspirational and intriguing, helping us to better 'witness' our actions and thoughts, and listen to our instincts and teachers."
—**KRISTIN OLSON**, founder of Urban Yoga Center Palm Springs

"Geoffrey Jowett's integrative approach to the physical, emotional, mental, and spiritual aspects of being will help healthcare practitioners communicate with their patients, and aid people to achieve their spiritual goals."
—**KAREN S. BLOCH**, DC, MS, ATC, CSCS, PES; USA Water Polo, Sports Medicine & Performance Coordinator; Bloch Chiropractic, Complete Koncepts co-owner

"The Power of I AM is a clear, concise, and comprehensible description of subtle energy. Easy to read, it provides a wonderful introductory overview for the spiritual seeker who is new to the concept of energy centers in the human body."
—**JOHN SCARINGE**, President and CEO, Southern California University of Health Sciences

"A beautiful expression for healing and heightening one's awareness. Geoffrey Jowett's gentle yet powerful approach assists the reader in understanding the power we behold as energetic beings."
—**SHELLY WILSON**, author of 28 Days to a New YOU, Connect to the YOU Within, and Journey into Consciousness

"Never has a book of this nature been needed more . . . A universal toolbox that is compelling and powerful."
—**DR. ADAM W. WACKER**, Doctor of Chiropractic, Lancaster, WI

"A beautifully written and illustrated exploration into the landscape of the chakras. This book is in my yoga backpack always."
—**JOHNNY YUHAS**, Yoga Teacher

The Power of I AM

ALIGNING THE CHAKRAS OF CONSCIOUSNESS

GEOFFREY JOWETT

AuthorHouse™
1663 Liberty Drive
Bloomington, IN 47403
www.authorhouse.com
Phone: 833-262-8899

Because of the dynamic nature of the Internet, any web addresses or links contained in this book may have changed since publication and may no longer be valid. The views expressed in this work are solely those of the author and do not necessarily reflect the views of the publisher, and the publisher hereby disclaims any responsibility for them.

Any people depicted in stock imagery provided by Getty Images are models, and such images are being used for illustrative purposes only.
Certain stock imagery © Getty Images.

This book is a work of non-fiction. Unless otherwise noted, the author and the publisher make no explicit guarantees as to the accuracy of the information contained in this book and in some cases, names of people and places have been altered to protect their privacy.

This book is printed on acid-free paper.

ISBN: 978-1-6655-2233-5 (sc)
ISBN: 978-1-6655-2234-2 (e)

Print information available on the last page.

Published by AuthorHouse 04/12/2021

CONTENTS

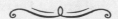

*"As far as we can discern,
the sole purpose of human existence is to kindle
a light in the darkness of mere being."*

—CARL JUNG

INTRODUCTION

The intention of *The Power of I AM: Aligning the Chakras of Consciousness* is to help you to appreciate the magnificence of your energy body, and familiarize you with ways to balance and align your energy systems. This book was deliberately written in the first person, to encourage you to read and energetically declare these words out loud as affirmations. The intention of stating "I AM" is faithfully affirming that you are one with the Source of Universal Consciousness, the Supreme Being. The precise text is presented succinctly for ease of use and convenience. It is my hope that when reading these words, you can resonate with a higher frequency, and your consciousness will harmonize with truth.

The prayers and affirmations, italicized in the text, were inspired through higher consciousness with the intentions of encouraging you and clarifying your purpose. You may wish to recite them out loud to increase the force and intensity from your being.

You are born with the wonderful gift of free will to choose and select your thoughts, words, and actions. The expression of yourself reflects the level of awareness of the situation you are manifesting into your reality. Your consciousness is that invisible part of you that realizes the true essence of your being. Your consciousness is more than your mind, for it encompasses the feelings within your heart center, the sensations and sentiments of your emotional centers, and the ideas and contemplations of your thought centers.

You are consciousness! As consciousness you have the awareness of higher self, the seeing eye of your soul, and you have the power to change the expression of who you are. Your power to change and shift the reality of your existence is expressed through the seven major energy centers of consciousness, called **chakras.**

As you will see in this book, your lower three chakras are the energy centers that allow you to shift and transform your emotional consciousness. Emotionally, you express through your emotional chakras how you nurture yourself, allow abundance and pleasure into your life, and calibrate your sense of worth and value in relationships.

The center of your universe is your heart chakra. It allows you to develop and convey your beliefs, and generates your feelings about all aspects of your being. Your heart chakra is your divine and sacred energy center for you to give, receive, and express love, compassion, and kindness.

Your upper three chakras are the energy centers that allow you to shift and transform your thought consciousness. You express how you speak your truth, recognize your inner knowing, and connect with your higher self through your thought chakras.

The seven energy-transforming chakra centers are conveyed in this book as levels of consciousness, utilizing the teachings of the archetypes of Carl Jung. Your aspiration, as a being of the energy universe, is to maintain a balanced and harmonizing continuous flow of energy through each of your chakras. Your free will choices influence the flow of energy within and through each energy-transforming center.

The Power of I AM: Aligning the Chakras of Consciousness aims to help you maintain a steady and balanced level of energy vibrations through each of your seven chakras so that you may be in harmony with love, peace, and joy. By providing you with the knowledge that the essence of your being is a fully integrated energy system of consciousness, this book can help you to achieve your greatest potential. Each vibrating energy level contributes to your divine existence and perfect resonance of light. To harmonically align each energetic layer collectively, as a whole, is to bring balance, peace, and joy to your awareness so that you may know Heaven.

The Light in You

There is a light that this world cannot give.
Yet you can give it, as it was given you.
And as you give it, it shines forth to call you from the world and follow it.
For this light will attract you As nothing in this world can do.

Ask for light
And learn that you are light.

—A COURSE IN MIRACLES

The Human Energy Being

"We live at the threshold of a universal recognition that the human being is not mere matter, but a potent, energetic field of consciousness. Modalities of the past millennium are quickly giving away to breakthrough technologies wherein we heal ourselves at the level of all true healing, which is spirit."

—MICHAEL BECKWITH

UNIVERSAL ENERGY FIELD

Universal Energy Field

The universe is a dynamic, fluid, interconnected,
and inseparable network of energy patterns
Everything in the universe is energy that vibrates at
various frequencies. Matter and energy
are interconvertible and interconnected.
Earth, water, fire, air, sound, light, and cosmic consciousness
are all energy forms, expressed within my energy being.

*I AM a vibration of the energetic universal field. I contribute to
the harmonic pulsation of the whole of creation.*

Package of Energy

I AM a package of quantum energy
within the totality of the universal energy
field! There are different levels of
consciousness that interpenetrate each
other within my human energy field.

*I AM so much more then my physical
body! I AM a gift of the universe.*

Luminous Aura

I have a luminescent multilayered energetic sphere that radiates from my body and interacts with the atmosphere that surrounds me.

I AM a perfect electromagnetic field that attracts like vibrations and repels opposing energies.

Energy Transformer

As part of the universe, I have the unique ability to recognize, perceive, process, and, most importantly, transform energy.

I AM able to transform energy using my free will to perceive and respond to the stimuli in my external environment. I AM a being of conscious energy!

Open Energy System

As an open system, *I AM a vibrational being
continuously exchanging energy with my environment.* My
environment can influence my energy field,
but not to the extent that my perceptions of
the external environment (people, places,
and situations) affect my energy being.

HUMAN ENERGY FIELD

Human Energy Field

My human organism is a series of interacting
multidimensional energy fields with
different levels of consciousness that are
parallel to one another and interconnected.
A dynamic, vibrating energy field
present within and around my physical
body moves in predictable patterns.

Energy Circulation

Energy is circulated through my body along definable pathways like the branches of arteries and veins within my circulatory system. My thoughts, feelings, emotions, and actions influence the circulation of energy in thousands of energy pathways called **meridians**, which run throughout my energy being.

Branching Energy Channels

Meridians are energy channels for circulating my life force, chi or prana. Energy circulates through my major energy centers or chakras and branches out into smaller energy channels or meridians, like the branches of a tree. There are twenty major energy channels that branch out from the central core of my energy body.

Twelve Standard Meridians

Another energy system affecting the well being of my body, mind, and spirit is made up of the energy meridians. There are twelve standard meridians divided into yin and yang groups that are specifically associated with every major organ of my body (heart, lungs, spleen, stomach, kidneys, liver, gallbladder, bladder, and large and small intestine).

Eight Extraordinary Meridians

The eight extraordinary meridians are
considered to be storage vessels or reservoirs
of energy and are not associated with my
internal organs. These energy channels
are referred to as the **spiritual axis**.

Energetic Harmony

My assignment is to keep my human energy field in balance, equilibrium, and harmony with the universal energies that surround me. My normal healthy body has a continuous flow of balanced energy circulating through and within it.

I AM the ruler of my kingdom of energy!

Energetic Discord

Energetic blockages and imbalances can
create mental, physical, emotional and/or
spiritual "dis-ease," or energetic conflict,
and resistance within my energy body.
Resistance is in opposition to the natural
flow of energy through my energy body.
Physical injuries and emotional traumas can
lower the efficiency of energy circulation
within my being and bring about long-
term changes in my energy field.

THE HUMAN SYMPHONY

The Human Symphony

My energetic body is composed of
superimposed layers of vibrational
frequencies of energy, all within the same
space. These energy layers, listed
from lower to higher frequencies, are:
physical body, etheric body, emotional
body, intellectual body, and soul body.

I AM a symphony of harmonious energies.

The Physical Vibration

My physical body provides the experience of pure separation from all others in the universe, which helps clarify my personal character and the essence of my individuality. It provides a stable, solid foundation for my energy body, the energetic skeleton of my energy body, and assists in the crystallization of consciousness. Containing five physical sensory organs — sight, touch, taste, hearing, and smell — my physical body helps me to perceive and respond to the world I live in.

Etheric Vibration

My etheric or vital body is the chi, prana,
or electromagnetic field around my
physical body, that connects it with my
higher energy bodies. As one of my subtle
bodies, my etheric body is the foundation
of organized life, and it provides vitality,
health, life, and orderliness to my physical
body. Aligning my consciousness to
the idea that I AM an energy being, my
etheric body slows down the energies from
my higher, subtle energy bodies to the
lower vibrations of my physical body.

Emotional Vibration

My emotional or astral body is a subtle body made up of all my emotions. Within my emotional body I fully experience, express, and repress all my sentiments, from fear, hate, and sorrow to love, happiness, and ecstasy. My dreams, fantasies, hallucinations, out-of-body experiences, near-death experiences, and visions are all housed within my being at this vibration. My emotional body offers me the ability to have desires from selfishness to selflessness, engages my imagination, and allows me to apply lower psychic abilities.

Intellectual Vibration

My intellectual body, or mental body, is also one of my subtle bodies composed of all my thoughts. It facilitates my cognition (knowing) and my ability to discern, have thoughts, beliefs, and concepts, and allows for me to apply my higher psychic abilities. All my thoughts from judgment, mental fear, and depression to compassion, understanding, peace, and joy are processed within my intellectual body. My thoughts are not just subjective; rather they have an existence apart from my brain within my intellectual body.

Soul Vibration

My soul, or causal body, is the repository
of the sum total of my lifetime experiences
gained through successive incarnations,
and acts as a vehicle of my ego; the real
thinking being of myself. It is the true
soul consciousness of my higher self and
contains all of my abstract ideas, higher
ideals, the accumulation of the good I
have achieved in each life, and past life
memories. The remembrances of my traits,
qualities, virtues, passions, attitudes, and
shortcomings acquired in past incarnations
are housed within this highest vibration
of my energy body. My soul body is
permanent and indescribable, and lasts
as long as the evolution of my being.

The Chakras

Chakra Energy Centers

There are seven major specialized energy centers, called **chakras**, in my subtle bodies that are interconnected to one another along the midline of my body. Chakras are clockwise spinning vortexes, or wheels of energy, associated with major nerve and glandular centers in my physical body.

My chakras are the super highways of
energy transference within my being.

Energy Awareness Centers

My chakras are energetic centers of
consideration and awareness that I use to
create and manifest my consciousness.

I AM the awareness of existence.
I AM a being of energy that knows myself
through the consciousness of my chakras.

Energy Transformers

My chakras act as transformers to decrease subtle energies from my higher energy bodies and translate them into physical responses (hormonal, nerve, and cellular). The integration of the mental, emotional, and spiritual energies occurs within my chakras, and they influence and affect my physical body (i.e., the holy grail of the mind, body, and soul connection).

I AM a physical, emotional, intellectual, and spiritual being! Each aspect of my being influences one another.

Unified Energy System

My choice of emotions, thoughts, and
beliefs influences the vibrational flow of
energy transformed within my chakras.
My chakras are interconnected; each
impacts the vibration of the others
and directly determines the harmonic
expression of my total energy being.

*I AM a harmonic pulsation of my
emotions, thoughts, and beliefs.*

Transforming Toward Heaven

My purpose as an energy being is to align myself with universal consciousness. Through the choices I make, I influence the circulation of energy through my chakras, which in turn affects the level of consciousness I express.

I AM aligning my emotions, thoughts, and feelings toward the love, peace, and joy of the higher consciousness of Heaven.

Emotional Energy Transformers

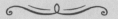

Root Chakra

Sacral Chakra

Solar Plexus Chakra

*Emotions are the conscious experiences
of the physical plane that result in
biological reactions and mental
awareness within my energy body.*

*"Let's not forget that the little emotions are the great
captains of our lives and we obey them without realizing it."*

—VINCENT VAN GOGH

ROOT CHAKRA ALIGNMENT

Root Chakra

The root chakra is located at the base of the spine, behind the sex organs, and is associated with my lower extremities (legs, feet, ankles, and toes). On a physical level, my root chakra is related to my skeletal and lymphatic systems and the functions of my adrenal glands. My root resonates and aligns with the color red, the element earth, and in the key of C.

Functions of the
Root Chakra

The root chakra grounds my spirit in the material world, and channels energy to the higher centers within my energy body. It is related to my instincts, security, and survival. The wisdom of the root chakra involves a sense of belonging to my physical family and the group safety, security, and survival within my family.

The root is my energetic pedestal on which every one of my body systems relies for stability and strength. My connection with Mother Earth and my own physical body is established through my root chakra.

My root chakra governs: security and earthly needs of my physical body, sensuality and survival instincts of my emotional body, stability and perceptions of my intellectual body, and spiritual security and safekeeping of my soul body.

Within my survival center I obtain courage, recognize my basic instincts to be resourceful, and have the will to survive and flourish. My root connects me to the spiritual energies of my ancestors and their memories. Within these ancestral memories are the physical survival threats and challenges of my soul family.

The Hopeless Victim Consciousness

The victim consciousness creates a belief that I am incapable of making choices that can best serve me. I feel hopeless in having very limited control of my destiny or fate. In this lower vibrational awareness, I see myself as vulnerable and I experience a state of helplessness because I believe that others can control and manipulate me. Also, as the victim, I feel as though I owe everyone more than I deserve for myself, or that they owe me. As a victim, I possess emotional feelings of fear, stress, and worry, and I am disconnected from divine Mother Earth.

Imbalanced Root Chakra

An imbalanced root chakra can result in feelings of insecurity, desperation, and isolation, with the idea that I am unable to manage my physical needs, and I am incapable of achieving my goals.

If I have excessive energy in my root chakra, I can be aggressive, bossy, domineering, and egocentric. I can adopt addictions and materialism.

If I have deficient energy in my root chakra, I can lack confidence, feel insecure, or I can be anxious with fear. Lower vibrational root energies can cause me to suffer with depression. With a lack of willpower and no discipline to achieve my goals, I can become disorganized and indulge in self-pity.

Dysfunctions in my root chakra can result in disorders in my skeletal system (e.g., osteoporosis, osteoarthritis, rickets, and bone cancer), lymphatic system (e.g., Hodgkin's and non-Hodgkin's lymphoma, lymphedema, lymphangitis, lymphatic filariasis, and other immune-related disorders), and eliminatory systems (e.g., colon and rectal cancer, polyps, colitis, irregular bowel movement, constipation, and diarrhea). Problems with my bones, teeth, legs, and feet can also be associated with instability in my root chakra. Emotional imbalances can include: resisting the present and holding on to the past; deep grief, anger, hatred, or resentment; and fears of abandonment or not being able to take care of my physical needs.

Balanced Root Chakra

A balanced and harmonized root chakra provides me with proper vitality and good health for my physical body. I feel a sense of being, grounded and centered, and in control of my life, trusting the world I live in.

I AM courageous, strong willed, confident, caring, and healthy when my root chakra is aligned.

THE NURTURING MOTHER

The Nurturing Mother Consciousness

Mother consciousness has the ability to allow me to take care of myself and to nurture my life force. I am comfortable recognizing and administering to my own physical needs and I can manage my own security and safety. Deeply rooted and grounded in the earth, my mother consciousness promotes self-love and the nurturing of others.

I AM aware, and provide for my own physical and emotional needs.

Root Chakra Prayer

Great Mother Earth consciousness, bestow
upon me your divine wisdom;

Align me with your blessings, so that I
may be attentive to my needs.

Thank you for your abundant offerings
to fulfill my necessities;

And for providing me with the awareness
of my emotional needs.

I offer blessings and gratitude for rooting
my life force to your divine graces.

Forever preserve my connection to your nurturing love.

Sincerely I give appreciation for all your
gracious and caring influence.

Root Chakra Gemstones

Red and black gemstones are associated with my root chakra, aligning me with security, stability, and safety. The gemstones that harmonize and balance my root chakra include: Apache tears, black agate, black kyanite, black tourmaline, garnet, hematite, obsidian, onyx, red carnelian, red jasper, red tourmaline, and ruby stone.

Red Flowers to
Awaken the Mother

Brilliant red blossoms to awaken my
nurturing mother awareness include:
alstroemeria, amaryllis anemone, anthurium,
geraniums, gerbera daisies, ginger,
gladiola, peony ranunculus, red carnations,
red lilies, red roses, and red tulips.

Healing Approaches to Energize the Root

All forms of physical exercise like walking,
swimming, running, biking, and playing
sports help energize my root chakra.
Activities like gardening, walking in
nature, and swimming in natural bodies
of water ground my root to Mother
Earth. Therapeutic touch, massage, and
all forms of body contact can help me
to reconnect to my physical body.

Yoga Poses to Open the Root Chakra

Beneficial yoga poses to open my root chakra
are those that encourage my connection to
the earth and keep me rooted and grounded.

Mountain, Tadasana

Warrior, Virabhadrasana I

Corpse, Savana

Music to Harmonize
the Root Chakra

Musical vibrations in the key of C help
to energize and align my root chakra.

Beethoven's Symphony no. 1, op. 21

Bizet's Symphony in C

Haydn's Symphony nos. 2, 30, 37, and 48

Mozart's Symphony no. 41, "Jupiter"

Prokofiev's Symphony no. 4

Schumann's Symphony no. 2, op. 61

Stravinsky's Symphony in C

Wagner's Symphony in C major

Root Energy Affirmations

*I nurture my life force with the loving
blessings from the Great Mother.*

*I take responsibly to provide myself
with security, safety, and love.*

*I am grounded, balanced, and centered
with a sense of well-being.*

*I am deeply connected to my physical nature, and I
allow my inner being to be satisfied and grounded.*

*I am aligned with the nurturing life
force of the Great Mother.*

SACRAL CHAKRA
ALIGNMENT

Sacral Chakra

The sacral chakra is located in the pelvic region of my body, at the center of the abdominal area, and is associated with my pelvis and lower back. On a physical level, my sacral chakra is related to my reproductive and urinary systems and the functions of my ovaries (females)/ testes (males). My sacral chakra resonates and aligns with the color orange, the element water, and in the key of D.

Functions of the
Sacral Chakra

My deep emotional responses are developed and registered in my sacral chakra and I explore and enjoy my beingness. This chakra is influenced by my emotions and centers me on the boundaries of delight, abundance, happiness, and the sexual pleasure I desire in my life. The wisdom of the sacral chakra helps me to understand what will enhance my life with abundance and pleasure.

My sacral chakra governs: the reproductive abilities of my physical body, joy and pleasures of my emotional body, desires and creativity of my intellectual body, and spiritual enthusiasm of my soul body.

My sacral chakra allows me to experience
the passions of each moment and accept the
conditions of my life. This is the center of my
creativity, emotions, sensuality, and intimacy.
The wisdom of my sacral chakra helps me to
experience my life through my feelings and
sensations and to seek passion, pleasure,
and enjoyment in life. It helps me to control
my level of contentment with the things
that bring me pleasure and fulfillment.

The Suffering Martyr Consciousness

In the martyr consciousness, I tend
to relinquish any satisfaction of myself and do
not allow for personal happiness or peace.
Suffering with self-pity, I focus on the
need to rescue and fix others. I do not feel
empowered or worthy of receiving love or
joy, and I am full of misery because of my
pessimistic attitudes and beliefs about the
world and myself. As the martyr, I accept
painful sacrifice and sympathy for myself,
which can lead me to feeling shameful, guilty,
and resentful about sacrificing for others.

Imbalanced Sacral Chakra

An imbalanced sacral chakra can result in me feeling emotional distress, withdrawn and indecisive in my day-to-day decisions. I can deprive myself of enjoyment, and lack creativity in my life when my sacral chakra is in disharmony.

If I have excessive energy in my sacral chakra I can be excessively sensitive and emotional, aggressive, overambitious, manipulative, overindulgent with pleasure addictions, and obsessed with sex.

If I have deficient energy in my sacral chakra, I can be oversensitive, timid, resentful, distrusting of others, feel a sense of guilt, become depressed, and isolate myself from others. My social skills are poor and I deny myself pleasure, passion, or excitement with an energy deficiency in my sacral chakra.

Dysfunctions in my sacral chakra can result in disorders in my urinary system (e.g., bladder, kidney, and prostate cancer; bladder and kidney stones; bladder infection; enlarged prostate; chronic renal failure; urethritis; and cystitis) and reproductive system (e.g., infertility; sexually transmitted diseases; endometriosis; menstrual problems; ovarian cysts; and testicular, ovarian, cervical, and uterine cancer). Problems associated with the sex organs (uterus and ovaries in females/testes in males) are linked to instability in my sacral chakra. Emotional imbalances can include: self-punishment and denial of my own needs; guilt, shame, rejection, and embarrassment; and blaming, conflict, and having anger toward others.

Balanced Sacral Chakra

A balanced and harmonized sacral
chakra allows me to be in touch with
my emotions and to be trusting toward
others. My emotional intelligence allows
for me to recognize and appreciate the
pleasurable experiences in my life and I
accept the abundance that is gifted to me.
There is a great sense of contentment
with my life because I have the ability to
experience delight and contentment.

*I AM happy, sociable, independent, constructive,
energetic, and enthusiastic about my life.*

THE PLEASURABLE EMPEROR/EMPRESS

The Pleasurable
Emperor/Empress Consciousness

The emperor/empress archetype allows
for beautiful and good things to be a part of my life.
By bringing pleasurable and joyful experiences into my
life, the emperor/empress consciousness
allows for me to be comfortable with
abundance, prosperity, success, and
personal happiness. My life is playful and
fun when I accept a balanced approach
to earthly pleasures and the freedom
to accept the wonders of the world.

*I AM celebrating an enjoyable life of abundant
pleasures and gratifying experiences.*

Sacral Chakra Prayer

Jubilant emperor consciousness,
I accept your joyful nature.

Bless me with an abundance of
compassion and comfort.

May I recognize the earthly pleasures
that best serve my soul,

And prosperous understandings
to fulfill my purpose.

I acknowledge all the generosities offered to me.

Satisfy me with gratitude for all
prosperity and success.

Allow for an enjoyable life to bring me
personal happiness.

Sacral Chakra Gemstones

Orange and orange-red gemstones are associated with my sacral chakra, aligning me with abundance and pleasure. The gemstones that harmonize and balance my sacral chakra include: amber, citrine, fire agate, fire opal, orange calcite, orange carnelian, orange jasper, peach selenite, sunstones, and topaz.

Orange Flowers to
Awaken the Emperor/Empress

Bright orange blossoms to awaken my abundant and pleasing emperor/empress awareness include: alstroemeria, bird of paradise, California poppy, cosmos, daylily, lion's tail, orange garden mum, orange snapdragon, orange tulips, pomegranate, rose orange climber, tea roses, tiger lily, and trumpet vine.

Healing Approaches to Energize the Sacral Chakra

Maintaining a gratitude journal, self-reflection on my daily pleasures, and prayers of appreciation align me to the emperor/empress awareness. Sending cards or electronic messages, or phoning family and friends to offer thanks for their participation in my life energizes my sacral chakra. Buying flowers, chocolates, or a special little gift for others and myself awakens my emperor/empress consciousness. Gifting myself the pleasures of a spa treatment, massage, bubble bath, haircut, or a nice meal at a favorite restaurant reminds me that I honor and respect myself.

Yoga Poses to Open
the Sacral Chakra

Beneficial yoga poses to open my sacral chakra are those that work with movement in my hips and lower abdomen, and allow energy to move through my sacral region.

Dancer's pose, Natarajasana

Child's pose, Balasana

Twisting triangle, Trikonasana

Music to Harmonize
the Sacral Chakra

Musical vibrations in the key of D help energize and align my sacral chakra.

Beethoven's Symphony no. 2, op. 36

Brahms's Symphony no. 2, op. 73

Haydn's Symphony nos. 53, 96, and 104

Mozart's Symphony nos. 7, 31, and 38

Prokofiev's Symphony no. 1

Rachmaninoff's Prelude in D major

Schubert's Symphony nos. 1 and 3

Tchaikovsky's Symphony no. 3

Sacral Energy Affirmations

I have gratitude for all the abundance
and pleasure in my life.

I am prosperous in every aspect of my life.

I appreciate all the joy and beauty gifted to me today.

I am grateful for the joyful people
and delightful experiences that bring
amusement to every moment of my life.

I am abundantly blessed with the
pleasurable gifts of life.

SOLAR PLEXUS CHAKRA
ALIGNMENT

Solar Plexus Chakra

The solar plexus chakra is located in
the abdominal region of my body and is
associated with my internal organs. On
a physical level, my solar plexus chakra is
related to my digestive and immune systems,
and the functions of my pancreas. My solar
plexus resonates and aligns with the color
yellow, the element fire, and in the key of E.

Functions of the
Solar Plexus Chakra

My solar plexus regulates the use of my energy and my ability to transform energy with my sense of self-esteem, self-worth, and confidence. The wisdom of the solar plexus chakra relates to my willpower and decision-making capabilities, and gives me the power and ability to shape my life in an effective way. I learn the lessons of my ego and personality in this area, and I am motivated to bring about change within my life. All that I think, feel, say, and do is an expression of the value I project of myself. The solar plexus chakra is my relationship center and the energy I receive and share with others is exchanged and transformed here.

My solar plexus chakra governs: the
digestion and nutritional processing of my
physical body, expansiveness and self-image
of my emotional body, personal power
of my intellectual body, and all matters
of spiritual growth of my soul body.

I meet my challenges with discipline,
confidence, and reliability through my
solar plexus center of empowerment. I use
and apply my personal power, especially in
my relationships, through recognizing the
authoritative warrior awareness within me.

The Powerless Servant Consciousness

The servant consciousness makes me feel undervalued and worthless. Others easily influence me, as I perceive them as having more power. I relinquish my personal power and my emotional needs because I do not believe I deserve what is best for me. In the awareness of the servant, I have low self-esteem and I depend on the approval of others who can easily control and manipulate me. I lack self-respect and do not value who I am when I accept this lower vibrational awareness.

Imbalanced Solar Plexus Chakra

An imbalanced solar plexus chakra can result in me feeling paranoia, having fear toward others, or the sense that I can be easily hurt or controlled by others. Often, I have a fear of being rejected, which can cause anger, irrational behavior, and in extreme cases an inferiority complex.

If I have excessive energy in my solar plexus chakra I can be judgmental, a workaholic, a perfectionist, and resentful toward authority. I can get overly aggressive, arrogant, stubborn, manipulative, extremely ambitious, and competitive when my solar plexus is over energized.

If I have deficient energy in my solar plexus chakra I can be depressed, insecure, fearful of others, and lack self-confidence. My willpower is weak and therefore I blame others for my own shortcomings

when I accept the servant awareness. I
get passive, sluggish, emotionally cold,
and lack self-discipline with energetic
deficiencies in my solar plexus chakra.

Dysfunctions in my solar plexus chakra
can result in disorders of my digestive
system (e.g., ulcers; stomach, intestinal,
pancreatic, and liver cancer; Crohn's disease;
pancreatitis; diabetes; hepatitis; bulimia;
celiac disease; gallstones; and cirrhosis)
and immune system (e.g., AIDS, lupus,
allergies, asthma, hives, and rheumatoid
arthritis). Problems associated with digestion
and the skin are also linked to instability in
my solar plexus chakra. Emotional imbalances
can include: fear, rejection, dread; feeling
overpowered and overwhelmed; a sense of
self-hate, anger, or bitterness; condemnation
of self and others; and powerlessness,
hopelessness, failure, and shame.

Balanced Solar Plexus Chakra

A balanced and harmonized solar plexus chakra allows me to be confident, outgoing, empowered, practical, spontaneous, flexible, humorous, alert, and optimistic. I feel tranquil and in harmony with my inner being and sense my unity and oneness with all humanity when this chakra is in alignment. In my relationships, a balanced solar plexus chakra allows me to be responsible, confident, funny, and respectful.

I AM empowered with respect and honor for myself. All that I do is a reflection of the value I have for myself.

THE EMPOWERED WARRIOR

The Empowered Warrior Consciousness

The warrior consciousness empowers me with confidence, and I can make effective and healthy decisions to take control of my life. I align with the empowered warrior archetype to be responsible, optimistic, and enthusiastic about developing my own personal power. I take control of my life and assertively make decisions that demonstrate self-respect and the value I have for myself.

I AM a warrior and stand up for myself.
I believe in myself and appreciate who I AM.

Solar Plexus Chakra Prayer

Confident warrior consciousness,
I admire your power.

Allow me to recognize my
boundless belief in myself.

Help me to know my divine right
and sacred significance.

Empower me with the realization
of my self-worth.

Bless me with opportunities to
honorably express myself.

Responsibly I stand up for myself with
my revered abilities.

I enthusiastically believe in
my own personal power.

Solar Plexus Chakra Gemstones

Yellow and yellow-green gemstones are associated with my solar plexus chakra, aligning me with self-respect. The gemstones that harmonize and balance my solar plexus chakra include: citrine, orange carnelian, sunstone, tiger's eye, yellow apatite, yellow calcite, yellow jasper, and yellow topaz.

Yellow Flowers to Awaken
the Warrior

Vibrant yellow flowers to awaken my confident warrior awareness include: arnica, balsamroot, black-eyed Susan, buttercup, coreopsis, daffodil, dahlia, dandelion, daylily, goldenrod, Graham Thomas rose, iris, marigold, Missouri primrose, pansy, prickly pear, rockrose, sunflower, and yarrow.

Healing Approaches to Energize the Solar Plexus Chakra

Physical exercises such as jogging, swimming, weight training, judo, aikido, yoga, and weight lifting help me awaken my inner confident warrior. Completion of my personal goals, finishing home, work, or personal projects, offering community service, and teaching others about empowerment help me to energize my solar plexus chakra.

Yoga Poses to Open the Solar Plexus Chakra

Beneficial yoga poses to open my solar plexus chakra are those that strengthen my core, and make me feel more powerful and confident.

Warrior, Virabhadrasana I

Warrior II, Virabhadrasana II

Bow, Dhanurasana

Music to Harmonize
the Solar Plexus Chakra

Musical vibrations in the key of E help to
energize and align my solar plexus chakra.

Bach's Symphony op. 18, no. 5, w. c28

Bischoff's Symphony no. 1

Bruckner's Symphony no. 7

Haydn's Symphony nos. 12 and 29

Marqués's Symphony no. 1

Méhul's Symphony no. 4

Schmidt's Symphony no. 1

Solar Plexus
Energy Affirmations

I greatly honor who I am. I treat myself with respect.

I value who I am and confidently stand in my power.

I reclaim my personal power.

I recognize that I am worthy of the very best.

*I am worthy and accept all the universal blessings
graciously gifted to me on this perfect day.*

I am a powerful being of the universal life force.

Belief Energy Transformer

H e a r t   C h a k r a

A belief is my conviction and faith in a truth, and involves the culmination of both the emotions of my lower three chakras with the thoughts of my upper three chakras. The heart is the center of my universe and I have the ability to transform every experience to the highest and purest vibration of love.

"There is a life-force with your soul, seek that life. There is a gem in the mountain of your body, seek that mine. O traveler, if you are in search of that don't look outside, look inside yourself and seek that."

*—*RUMI

HEART CHAKRA
ALIGNMENT

Heart Chakra

The heart chakra is located at the center
of my chest, and is associated with my
chest, upper back, and upper extremities
(arms, wrists, hands, and fingers).
On a physical level, my heart chakra is
related to my circulatory, respiratory,
and immune systems and the functions
of my thymus gland. My heart chakra
resonates and aligns with the color green,
the element air, and in the key of F.

Functions of the
Heart Chakra

The heart chakra is my sacred core where I accept, share, and circulate love, compassion, tenderness and kindness. Housed within my heart center are the lessons of love and affection for others and myself, and the surrendering of anger and guilt to achieve the freedom of forgiveness. When my heart center is open, I can heal with wishes, hopes, and feelings of divine love.

My energetic focal point is my heart chakra and it radiates with love, joy, peace, and harmony. The most powerful vibrations within my energy body: my feelings and beliefs are generated through my heart, which is the center of my beingness, the center of my universe.

My heart chakra governs: the circulation
of my physical body, forgiveness and
unconditional love of my emotional body,
passions of my intellectual body, and
spiritual devotion within my soul body.

The sacred healing center of my being is
my heart chakra, because it moves love into
all aspects of my life to bring wholeness.
The compassionate energy and kindness
I have toward all life, and the unconditional
acceptance of others, come from the wisdom
of my heart chakra. I am aware of my
connection to Source and the essence of my
being as divine love through my heart center.

The Vulnerable Actor/Actress Consciousness

The actor/actress consciousness encourages me to believe that love is not real and should be feared. I am unable to get too close to others, incapable of real intimate and cherished relationships, and tend to feel vulnerable when giving or receiving acts of affection. By offering love based on conditions, and with expectations, I do not have the freedom to love for the sake of just being in the pure vibration of love. Actor/actress awareness often leads me to be resentful, unforgiving, remorseful, and incapable of releasing and healing past wounds of condition-based love.

Imbalanced Heart Chakra

An imbalanced heart chakra can result in losing my understanding of reality about my world and myself. Fear of love can result in low respect for myself, and self-doubt. Feeling hopeless, I constantly seek reassurance from others and feel vulnerable to the affections of others. I measure the love I give out compared to the love I receive in return, constantly judging.

If I have excessive energy in my heart chakra, I can be judgmental, demanding, critical, possessive, moody, and resentful. As the heart energy intensifies, I develop jealousy, possessiveness, and even codependency with others. I also am incapable of setting sensible and reasonable emotional boundaries in relationships.

If I have deficient energy in my heart chakra, I can be depressed, paranoid,

and indecisive, fear being rejected
or judged by others, and feel insecure with
a constant need of reassurance. Due
to fear, I am judgmental, opinionated,
and retreat to becoming antisocial,
withdrawn, shy, and intolerant of others.

Dysfunctions in my heart chakra can
result in disorders of my circulatory
system (e.g., coronary artery disease,
arrhythmia, cardiomyopathy, atherosclerosis,
angina, congenital heart disease, and
hypertension), respiratory system (e.g.,
asthma, bronchitis, COPD, pneumonia,
tuberculosis, emphysema, cystic fibrosis,
and lung cancer), and immune system
(e.g., AIDS, lupus, allergies, asthma, hives,
and other immune disorders). Problems
associated with circulation, respiration,
and immunity are also linked to instability in
my heart chakra. Emotional imbalances can
include: difficulty giving and receiving love;
desperation, fear, fatigue, misery, prolonged
grief, hopelessness, and intense sadness;
and hatred and resentment of others.

Balanced Heart Chakra

A balanced and harmonized heart chakra
allows me to have a sense of calming kindness
and tolerance for others. With compassion,
I have a desire to love and nurture others,
offering unconditional love and affection.
I openly receive and freely offer love
to everyone and everything; including
myself. I am romantic and generous in my
relationships and I am optimistic about
my life. I have a genuinely empathetic and
sympathetic heart with charity for all.

*I AM passionate about my life, and I live
in the present moment with love.*

THE COMPASSIONATE LOVER

The Compassionate Lover Consciousness

The lover consciousness is compassionate
awareness that love is the center of my
being and my universe, and love is found
in the present moment. I am
aware that the purpose of my being is to
perpetuate the love of Source and Creator.
When I recognize that love is the center of
my being, I become aware that giving and
receiving love are one in the same and of
equal value. The lover consciousness allows
me to freely love my life as it is, to freely love
myself, and to love for the sake of loving.

*I AM one with love. I generously love
myself freely and openly.*

Heart Chakra Prayer

Compassionate lover consciousness,
I embrace your caring affections.

Gratify my heart with thoughtful
understanding for all.

Satisfy me with sincere kindness
and consideration.

Allow me to believe in the
generosity of genuine love.

May I freely offer and openly
receive the friendship of love.

With cordial appreciation,
I love for the sake of loving.

I proclaim that love is
the essence of my being.

Heart Chakra Gemstones

Green and pink gemstones are associated with my heart chakra by aligning me with love, compassion, and kindness. The gemstones that harmonize and balance my heart chakra include: bloodstone, emerald, green adventurine, green kyanite, green moonstone, jade, malachite, moldavite, pink calcite, pink rhodochrosite, rhodonite, and rose quartz.

Green Flowers to Awaken
the Lover

Rejuvenating green flowers to awaken
my caring lover awareness include:
bells of Ireland, green carnation, green
chrysanthemum, green cymbidium, green
daylily, green gladiolus, green hellebore,
green rose, green zinnia, and orchids.

Healing Approaches to
Energize the Heart

Social activities that support friendship and kindred spirits are helpful to energize your heart chakra. Completing art projects, sharing music, romantic stories or poetry, comedy shows or movies, cooking and eating together and encouraging conversations all support a loving heart. Aligning with the stillness and beauty of nature through camping, hiking, sailing, swimming, and biking enriches loving kindness at your core. Artistic endeavors like painting, singing, drawing, poetry, and all other forms of creative expression can enhance the affectionate vibrations of love. Sharing love with someone in need, or simple acts of kindness can brighten all hearts.

Yoga Poses to Open
the Heart Chakra

Beneficial yoga poses for my heart
chakra are those that open my heart
center and invite love into my life.

Camel, Ushtrasana

Cobra, Bhujangasana

Forward bend, Uttanasana

Music to Harmonize
the Heart Chakra

Musical vibrations in the key of F help
energize and align my heart center.

Bach's Brandenburg Concertos nos. 1 and 2

Beethoven's Symphony 8 in F Major, op. 93

Brahms's Symphony 3 in F major, op. 90

Dvořák's Symphony no. 5

Mozart's Piano Concerto no. 19

Shostakovich's Piano Concerto no. 2

Vivaldi's Concerto no. 3 in F Major, op. 8

Heart Energy Affirmations

*I love myself unconditionally and
with no expectations.*

*I am open to receive love from all
those that offer it to me.*

Love is my purpose for being.

*I forgive the past and open my heart to
love. I am free and full of joy.*

*I am a compassionate occurrence
of universal love.*

Thought Energy Transformers

Throat Chakra

Third Eye Chakra

Crown Chakra

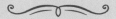

Thoughts and ideas are interpretations, representations, or predictions about the human experience. The reasoning and reflection of mental energies are processed through my upper three chakras.

"The energy of the mind is the essence of life."

—ARISTOTLE

THROAT CHAKRA
ALIGNMENT

Throat Chakra

The throat chakra is located at the base
of my throat, and is associated with
my throat, shoulders, jaw, and neck.
On a physical level, my throat chakra
is related to my upper respiratory and
upper digestive systems and the functions
of my thyroid gland. My throat chakra
resonates and aligns with the color blue,
the element sound, and in the key of G.

Functions of the
Throat Chakra

The throat chakra is related to expression and communication, and the use of my will to grow creatively through self-expression. It is the means by which I transmit and convey my thoughts, ideas, passions, and desires.

My throat chakra governs: the communication of my physical body, independence and self-expression of my emotional body, fluent thought and beliefs of my intellectual body, and spiritual will and security of my soul body.

The energy of my throat chakra allows
me to see beyond my doubts, fears, and
limitations associated with my cultural,
religious, and social upbringing. I am
inspired to creatively seek, share, and teach
truth and to stand up for what I believe in.
Teaching, coaching, and counseling, as well
as being genuine, original, and authentic
are the wise gifts of the throat chakra.

Communicating with sincere thoughts,
precise words, and creative actions
aligns me with integrity and honesty
in the expression of my being.

The Suppressed Silent Child Consciousness

The silent child consciousness suppresses my feelings, thoughts, and beliefs and remains closed with the fear that I might experience pain and sorrow. Repressing my feelings with a false sense of safety in silence makes me feel that if I speak my truth or act with integrity, I will be humiliated, rejected, reprimanded, or punished. As the silent child, I believe that no one listens to or cares about what I have to say, and I associate silence with compliance and speaking my truth as defiance. Many times, in accepting the silent child consciousness, I will lie to protect my fears and myself.

Imbalanced Throat Chakra

An imbalanced throat chakra can result in my inability to express my thoughts and feelings. Deceitfully, I can be unfaithful, self-righteous, untrustworthy, and cold. I am unable to truthfully express myself and I can be unimaginative and bored.

If I have excessive energy in my throat chakra I can be arrogant, boastful, deceitful, self-righteous, and talkative. I have poor listening skills, encourage gossip and cynical talking, and my words and actions do not complement each other.

If I have deficient energy in my throat chakra I can be timid, inconsistent, unreliable, devious, manipulative, disloyal, and untrustworthy. I am afraid to speak honestly and unable to freely and consistently express myself, especially my feelings to others.

Dysfunctions in my throat chakra can result in disorders of my upper respiratory (e.g., thyroid cancer, hyper- and hypothyroid disease, sinusitis, tonsillitis, pharyngitis, and laryngitis) and upper digestive systems (e.g., tongue and salivary gland disease, mouth ulcers, and gastroesophageal reflex disease/GERD). Problems associated with the upper respiratory and upper digestive tract are linked to instability in my throat chakra. Emotional imbalances can result in: a sense of being overwhelmed; repressing emotions, creativity, or self-expression; resentment of authority; fear of punishment or being persecuted; self-rejection; and frustration from not being able to communicate effectively.

Balanced Throat Chakra

A balanced and harmonized throat chakra will allow me to express myself directly, truthfully, caringly, and clearly in all situations. I speak truthfully from my higher self, make respectable decisions and provide ingenious ideas and innovative solutions. I can effectively communicate through hearing, speaking, and listening. My thoughts, words, and actions complement and support each other with integrity. I am a good listener and direct others to be honest and have integrity.

I AM ingenious, motivating, and encouraging.
I have the freedom to express the true
essence of my beliefs and myself.

THE TRUTHFUL COMMUNICATOR

The Truthful Communicator Consciousness

The communicator consciousness lets me speak openly and freely with clarity, honesty, and intention. Through creative and free expression, the communicator awareness allows me to have integrity with the alignment of my thoughts, words, and deeds. With sincerity and openness I creatively express my purpose, passion, and will.

I AM honest and speak from both my mind and heart.
I passionately stand up for what I believe in.

Throat Chakra Prayer

Magnificent communicator consciousness,
I freely speak my beliefs.

With liberty and divine right I state
my authentic truths.

To convey the promising intuitions
from my higher consciousness

With heartening intentions I share
my inspired feelings.

Allow me to openly express my ideas
with clarity and precision.

I express from the sincerity of my heart
and the integrity of my mind.

I encourage others with hopeful
words and faithful actions.

Throat Chakra Gemstones

Blue, blue-green, and blue-purple gemstones are associated with my throat chakra, aligning me with the truth, integrity, and honesty. The gemstones that harmonize and balance my throat chakra include: angelite, aquamarine, blue lace agate, blue topaz, blue calcite, blue celestine, blue sodalite, lapis lazuli, sapphire, and turquoise.

Blue Flowers to Awaken
the Communicator

Dynamic blue flowers to awaken my
truthful communicator awareness
include: asters, balloon flower, bellflower,
blue hydrangeas, blue roses, blue star,
bluestone perennial, brunnera, clematis,
delphinium, geraniums, grape hyacinth,
lead plant, morning glory, and salvia.

Healing Approaches to Energize the Throat

All forms of self-expression and
sharing my sincere thoughts, ideas, and
beliefs help energize my throat chakra.
Artistic activities like painting, drawing,
photography, singing, playing an instrument,
coloring, poetry, journaling, and writing,
performing events like acting, storytelling,
reciting poetry, dancing, teaching, and
coaching, and just being myself allow
me to be a true communicator.

Yoga Poses to Open the Throat Chakra

Beneficial yoga poses are those that open and strengthen my throat area.

Plow, Halasana

Fish, Matsyasana

Cobra, Bhujangasana

Music to Harmonize
the Throat Chakra

Musical vibrations in the key of G help
to energize and align my throat chakra.

CPE Bach's Symphony in G Wq 183/4

CPE Bach's String Symphony no. 1

JC Bach's Symphony op. 3
no. 6 in G major WC6

Dvořák's Symphony no. 9

Haydn's Symphony no. 94 "Surprise"

Mozart's Symphony no. 27

Mozart's Symphony no. 12, k.110

Throat Energy Affirmations

I openly and creatively express my truth. I am free.

I always speak with honesty and act with integrity.

*I listen to my inner voice, and I sincerely speak
with the wisdom and beauty of my heart.*

*I am a perfect expression of universal
truth and elegant grace.*

*I am a brilliant expression of
universal consciousness.*

THIRD EYE CHAKRA
ALIGNMENT

Third Eye Chakra

The third eye chakra is located at the center of my forehead, and is associated with my face and brain. On a physical level, my third eye chakra is related to my central nervous and endocrine systems, and the functions of the pineal gland. My third eye chakra resonates and aligns with the color indigo, the element light, and in the key of A.

Special note: Some believe that the pineal and pituitary glands should be exchanged in their relationships to the third eye and crown chakras. I have chosen to associate the pineal with the third eye, based on my study and my intuition. I believe the pineal gland is connected to the realm of thought and the inner knowing.

Functions of the Third Eye Chakra

The third eye chakra allows me to understand and analyze reality, and balances my lower and higher selves. Insightfully, I can process information and knowledge from my past memory, and project my future. Lessons of wisdom, knowledge, intuition, discernment, and my imagination are related to this chakra. Also, my gifts of clairvoyance (ability to visualize telephatically), clairsentience (ability to feel telephatically), and clairaudience (ability to hear telephatically) are associated with my third eye. Through the wisdom of the third eye chakra I can focus on my personality and my relationship to the universe by looking inward.

My third eye chakra governs: the
biological cycles of my physical body,
inner knowing of my emotional body,
imagination of my intellectual body, and
spiritual insights of my soul body.

The energies of my third eye allow me to
be mindful and to see both the outer and
inner worlds. Through self-reflection,
I receive clarity to access my inner
guidance that connects me to the depths
of my being. My insightful mind allows
me to access universal wisdom, so that
I recognize the synchronicity of life.

The Critical Intellectual Consciousness

The intellectual consciousness overintellectualizes, over-rationalizes, and is hypercritical about my life resulting in skepticism, confusion, and distress. I experience my life with theories, judgments, and mental analysis resulting in an internal mental imbalance and the misuse of my thinking abilities with an overstimulated mind. When I allow the lower vibration of intellectual consciousness, I have mechanical responses to my life and I suppress my feelings from my heart center.

Imbalanced Third Eye Chakra

An imbalanced third eye chakra can influence my mind to abandon reality and accept the realms of fantasy and delusion. My mind loses clarity and the efficiency to process my thoughts and I can become agitated, inconsiderate, overanalytical, and judgmental.

If I have excessive energy in my third eye chakra, I can be proud, arrogant, manipulative, egotistical, boastful, illogical, and irrational, and have limited concentration. I can develop hallucinations, nightmares, become obsessed, and have delusions.

If I have deficient energy in my third eye chakra, I can be nonassertive, passive, aloof, unable to distinguish between my ego self and my higher self, confused, and oversensitive to the feelings of others. My ability to visualize is clouded and I have a limited imagination, poor memory, and no or limited recollection of my dreams.

Dysfunctions in my third eye chakra can result in disorders of my nervous system (e.g., sight problems, cataracts, glaucoma, ear infections, deafness, brain tumors, migraines, Alzheimer's, dementia, stroke, seizures, meningitis, encephalitis, and epilepsy), and endocrine system (e.g., abnormal hormone levels resulting in imbalances in growth, maturation, digestion, metabolism, or reproduction). Memory issues, lack of concentration, and learning disabilities are linked to issues in my third eye chakra. Emotional imbalances can include: frustration and distraction problems when planning, concentrating or communicating; rejection, isolation and self-criticism; incorrect beliefs; self-centeredness and stubbornness; and being overwhelmed and unable to care.

Balanced Third Eye Chakra

A balanced and harmonized third eye chakra allows me to see clear visions and receive understandable messages from my subtle senses (psychic information). I lose my preoccupation with worldly events and material possessions. I experience higher consciousness, inner awareness, and peace of mind when I accept the intuitive consciousness. I take responsibility for all that I manifest and I recognize the influence of my mind to create.

I AM highly intuitive, insightful, imaginative, and clear-sighted. I AM wise.

THE WISE INTUITIVE

140

The Wise Intuitive Consciousness

The intuitive consciousness offers me the gift of insight, imagination, and wisdom to understand the essence of life. Freely accessing my deepest wisdom, the intuitive allows me the awareness of my inner knowing, which provides me guidance through life. I fully trust and accept the messages, insights, and wisdom provided to me and I recognize and believe in the synchronicity of my life.

I AM intuitive and I listen to my higher self. I AM one with universal mind.

Third Eye Chakra Prayer

*Wise intuitive consciousness, inspire me
with heavenly understanding.*

*Align me with the elegance and
divinity of universal mind.*

*Attune me to collective intelligence
of my inner knowing.*

*May I recognize and accept the
sacred insights gifted to me.*

*Inspire me with clear perceptions
and virtuous wisdom.*

*I offer gratitude for the precious
knowledge continuously provided.*

*Sensibly provide guidance that allows me to
realize the sacred synchronicity of life.*

Third Eye Gemstones

Clear, white, and purple gemstones are associated with my third eye chakra, aligning me with insight, wisdom, and inner knowing. The gemstones that harmonize and balance my third eye chakra include: amethyst, blue kyanite, blue tourmaline, cryolite, green fuchsite, herderite, labradorite, lepidolite, moldavite, and smoky quartz.

Indigo Flowers to
Awaken the Intuitive

Effervescent indigo flowers to awaken my
insightful intuitive awareness include:
Angelface blue angelonia, annual lobelia,
bearded iris, bellflowers, blue hibiscus,
garden sage, germander sage, indigo
mums, low dark blue iris, pansies, royal
candles, salvia, skyflower, and Veronica.

Healing Approaches to Energize the Third Eye

Higher consciousness channeling activities energize my third eye chakra and include: all forms of meditation, contemplation, and reflection, dream analysis, automatic writing, and inspirational speaking. Reading inspiring literature, attending spiritual lectures or workshops, journaling, praying, listening to inspirational music, reflecting on enlightening art, yoga, and contemplating the limitless beauty of nature all help awaken my inner knowing.

Yoga Pose that Open the Third Eye Chakra

Beneficial yoga poses to open the third eye are those that help me connect with my innermost self.

Thunderbolt, Vajrasana

Downward facing dog, Adho Mukha Shvansana

Sphinx, Salamba Bhujangasana

Music to Harmonize
the Third Eye Chakra

Musical vibrations in the key of A
energize and align my third eye center.

CPE Bach's String Symphony no. 4

Beethoven's Symphony no. 7, op. 92

Bruckner's Symphony no. 6

Haydn's Symphony nos. 59 and 64

Mendelssohn's Symphony no. 4

Mozart's Symphony no. 29

Shostakovich's Symphony no. 15, op. 141

Third Eye Energy Affirmations

I attune my consciousness to the
wisdom of my inner knowing.

My intuition allows me to make wise
choices that best serve my higher self.

I am open to receive divine guidance that
brings love, joy, and peace into my life.

I free myself from the illusions of the
world and accept wisdom about the deeper truths of life.

I am one with the magnificence
of universal intelligence.

CROWN CHAKRA
ALIGNMENT

Crown Chakra

The crown chakra is located on the top
of my head, and is associated with my
head, brain, and nervous system. On a
physical level, my crown chakra is related
to my nervous system and indirectly
to every other system in my body, and
the functions of my pituitary gland.
My crown resonates and aligns with
the color purple, the element cosmic
consciousness, and in the key of B.

Functions of the
Crown Chakra

The crown chakra is my connection to the whole of creation and to cosmic consciousness of life eternal. It is associated with pure consciousness and affects the functions of my higher brain. The crown chakra is related to my spiritual nature, inner beauty, and my connection with Divine Source.

It is through my crown chakra that I align with my higher consciousness and realize the soul purpose of my being. I embrace the law of unity and oneness, and the realization that Source and I are one. I am one with the universe. My crown unifies me with the awareness of my being as an infinite and eternal soul.

My crown chakra governs: the regulation of my physical body, hopes of my emotional body, convictions of my intellectual body, and spiritual karma of my soul body.

The energies of my crown chakra allow me to experience mystical unity and oneness with everything and everyone by connecting me to the Divine Source of all creation. I transcend my ego to be connected to the eternal wisdom of collective consciousness, and have a deep knowing that there is a universal order to all of existence. I realize my spiritual nature and sacred self.

The Arrogant Egotist Consciousness

The egotist consciousness encourages me to be proud and pompous with a narcissistic personality that focuses on self-gratification. It promotes resistance to developing my spiritual awareness and to accepting the idea that there is a power and purpose greater than myself. The ungrateful and self-indulging awareness of the egotist supports my belief that only I am responsible for my own personal achievement. Nothing has the ability, and no one has the authority, to immediately influence my life except me. The lonely and isolated feeling of the egotist consciousness establishes my proud fixation on the material world.

Imbalanced Crown Chakra

An imbalanced crown chakra can result in my mental confusion, coordination problems, instability, and feelings of alienation, exhaustion, boredom, or depression. A shadow of doubt over my whole energy system can occur with a state of disharmony in my crown.

If I have excessive energy in my crown chakra, I can be frustrated, resistant, arrogant, manipulative, illogical, and irrational. I can be confused, unfocused, and feel disassociated from my body when being overly intellectual.

If I have deficient energy in my crown chakra I can be indecisive, confused, lack passion and desire, nonassertive, passive, detached and distant, and have learning difficulties. I can become rigid in my beliefs, cynical toward my spiritual nature, materialistic, greedy, and want to dominate others.

Dysfunctions in my crown chakra result in disorders of my nervous system (e.g., amnesia, Parkinson's disease, psychosis, multiple personality disorders, neurosis, paralysis, learning disorders, and mental disorders) and endocrine system (e.g., dysfunctional hormone production that affects the growth and development of every organ in the body and regulation and metabolism of all major biological processes). Problems associated with the muscular and skeletal systems are linked to instability in my crown chakra. Indirectly, all diseases can be related to misalignment in my crown chakra. Emotional imbalances can result in: lack of self-understanding and direction; aggression; self-centeredness; and depression.

Balanced Crown Chakra

A balanced and harmonized crown chakra can allow me to understand things from a wider context with creativity, compassion, and an expansive imagination. As my mind quiets, I can become more focused and receive clear intuitive messages with a clear spiritual connection. The more balanced and stable my crown is, the more open I am to divine energy and universal consciousness.

I AM one with collective consciousness. With clarity
I AM opened to receive universal wisdom.

THE ENLIGHTENED GURU

The Enlightened Guru
Consciousness

The guru consciousness encourages me
to recognize the beauty and grace of my
spiritual nature, and fully connects me to
the awareness of my higher self.
Through my higher consciousness, the guru
awareness opens me to receive love and
wisdom. I can better master the wisdom of
the spiritual plane and accept the essence
of myself as divine love. My guru awareness
compassionately shares and teaches others
about their higher consciousness and love.

I AM the incarnation of Divine and
Eternal Source. I believe in the realm of
limitless possibilities and miracles.

Crown Chakra Prayer

*Gracious and pure guru consciousness, may
I realize my oneness with Source.*

*Help me to recognize the goodness
and beauty in all of creation.*

*With gratitude, I identify and accept the
limitless possibilities gifted to me.*

*My channels are open to receive the divine
and eternal wisdom of the ages.*

*May I master my spiritual nature and
achieve the awareness of higher self.*

*Allow me to accept and teach the wisdom of
the miracles of love, faith, and charity.*

*Enable me to know the I AM presence and
be the essence of Eternal Source.*

Crown Chakra Gemstones

Clear, white, and purple gemstones are associated with my crown chakra, aligning me with my spiritual nature and divinity. The gemstones that harmonize and balance my crown chakra include: ametrine quartz, atacamite, blue kyanite, clear crystal quartz, lavender quartz, lilac lepidolite, moonstone, purple amethyst, selenite, and seraphinite.

Purple Flowers to Awaken the Guru

Vibrant purple flowers to awaken my enlightened guru awareness include: African violet, aster, butterfly bush, clematis jackmanii, crocus, dahlia, delphinium, fan flower, heliotrope, impatiens, iris, lilacs, pansies, petunias, purple bee balm, purple hydrangea, purple pansies, rhododendron, thyme, Veronica, and wisteria.

Healing Approaches to Energize the Crown Chakra

Inspirational activities energize my crown chakra and include deep prayer and self-reflection in silence, meditation, contemplation, and automatic writing. I am connected to my higher consciousness when spending time in nature, sacred places, and with inspired people. Spiritual practices like yoga, Chi Qigong and Tai Chi, singing inspirational hymns, mantras and affirmations, chanting, drumming, and playing all instruments, and dancing under the stars all help connect me to universal consciousness.

Yoga Poses to Open
the Crown Chakra

Beneficial yoga poses calm, balance, and open my crown chakra and nourish my energies to awaken my higher self.

Half lotus, Ardha Padmasana

Headstand, Salamba Sirhasana

Corpse, Savasana

Music to Harmonize
the Crown Chakra

Musical vibrations in the key of B help to energize and align my crown chakra.

Haydn's Symphony no. 46

Korngold's Sinfonietta op. 5

Monn's Sinfonia in B major

Shostakovich's Symphony no. 2,
"To October," op. 14

Crown Energy Affirmations

*I am one with Source and all the
magnificence of the universe.*

*I channel universal wisdom to bring
peace, joy, and love to the world.*

*I attune to the highest and purest universal
vibrations of wisdom and compassion.*

*I openly receive universal wisdom and grace when
I AM connected to collective consciousness.*

I am one with the glory and splendor of Divine Source.

Chakra Atonement *and* Attunement

ATONEMENT AND ATTUNEMENT PRAYER

My Guides channeled an enlightening affirmation and prayer to help align and balance our chakras. It is suggested to declare each statement by speaking it out loud three times for the body, mind, and soul. The atonement (at-one-ment) declarations are for you to make amends to your higher self and God for reparations in believing that you are less than you truly are, a being of Source. The attunements are declarations to harmoniously convey and recognize your true God nature. Announce daily your intentions to be the divine and loving eternal being you are considered through your higher consciousness.

Root Chakra

ATONEMENT

I release the victim from my being!

I release the victim from my being!

I release the victim from my being!

ATTUNEMENT

I embrace the mother vibration, and nurture myself!

I embrace the mother vibration, and nurture myself!

I embrace the mother vibration, and nurture myself!

Sacral Chakra

ATONEMENT

I remove the martyr from my being!

I remove the martyr from my being!

I remove the martyr from my being!

ATTUNEMENT

I accept the abundance and pleasure of the emperor/empress!

I accept the abundance and pleasure of the emperor/empress!

I accept the abundance and pleasure of the emperor/empress!

Solar Plexus Chakra

ATONEMENT

I relinquish the servant from my being!

I relinquish the servant from my being!

I relinquish the servant from my being!

ATTUNEMENT

I value and respect the warrior that is within me!

I value and respect the warrior that is within me!

I value and respect the warrior that is within me!

Heart Chakra

ATONEMENT

I forgive the actor/actress and release him/her from my being!

I forgive the actor/actress and release him/her from my being!

I forgive the actor/actress and release him/her from my being!

ATTUNEMENT

*I allow affection, kindness, and compassion
to enhance the lover that I am!*

*I allow affection, kindness, and compassion
to enhance the lover that I am!*

*I allow affection, kindness, and compassion
to enhance the lover that I am!*

Throat Chakra

ATONEMENT

I release the silent child from my being!

I release the silent child from my being!

I release the silent child from my being!

ATTUNEMENT

*I speak with clarity and truth, and act with
the integrity of the communicator!*

*I speak with clarity and truth, and act with
the integrity of the communicator!*

*I speak with clarity and truth, and act with
the integrity of the communicator!*

Third Eye Chakra

ATONEMENT

I release the intellectual from my being!

I release the intellectual from my being!

I release the intellectual from my being!

ATTUNEMENT

I allow my inner knowing to manifest the miracles of the intuitive!

I allow my inner knowing to manifest the miracles of the intuitive!

I allow my inner knowing to manifest the miracles of the intuitive!

Crown Chakra

ATONEMENT

I surrender the ego of my being!

I surrender the ego of my being!

I surrender the ego of my being!

ATTUNEMENT

*I embrace the higher consciousness of the guru,
which makes me aware I am one with Source!*

*I embrace the higher consciousness of the guru,
which makes me aware I am one with Source!*

*I embrace the higher consciousness of the guru,
which makes me aware I am one with Source!*

Pure Consciousness

I AM more than my physical body.
I AM pure consciousness with the power to transform
any thought, feeling, emotion, word, or action
into the highest vibration of divine love.

Energetic Restoration

*I reclaim all the energies I have misplaced,
and empower my being to transform all my
consciousness toward the higher vibration of love,
joy, and peace. I AM love, joy, and peace!*

CELEBRATION OF TOTALITY

Celebration of Totality

I use this moment to commemorate my energy being for all the good it has done to service, honor, and safeguard the supreme belief that I AM universal consciousness. I AM the totality of Source's creation and I use my consciousness to transform universal energy toward love!

Closing Prayer

I AM the Universal Elements of Consciousness

I AM . . . the nurturing mother that
cultivates the provisions of the earth.

I AM . . . the abundant empress that satisfies
the thirst of each of my wishes.

I AM . . . the worthy warrior that ignites
the admired flame of reverence.

I AM . . . the lover that compassionately
breathes the breath of affection.

I AM . . . the honest communicator that
freely chants the sound of truth.

I AM . . . the insightful intuitive that shines
with the light of understanding

I AM . . . the heavenly guru that realizes
the glory of God is within myself.

ABOUT THE AUTHOR

Geof was raised in Upstate New York and since his childhood, he has had the ability to sense energy fields around living things and connect with the spiritual realm.

After he earned his MS in Cell and Molecular Biology from the University of Buffalo, Geof's career has led to ten years in biotechnology and fifteen years as a college biology instructor and dean.

Geof is an intuitive medium and spiritual educator. He has published two books on mediumship, *What's Cooking in Heaven Grandma and Hope for Parents Who Have Lost Children*, and a meditation CD called *Allowing Peace*.

It is his passion to write and teach about universal consciousness and the rediscovery of the higher self and the continuity of life. As an educator, Geof provides spiritual workshops on spirit communication, intuition development, channeling higher self, chakra balancing and healing, and karma and reincarnation throughout North America.

Geof resides in Palm Springs, California, where he offers mediumship, soul progression, and chakra balancing readings. To schedule a reading, set up a workshop in your area, or to learn more about Geof, please visit his website at www.geofjowett.com or email him at mediumgeof@yahoo.com.

ACKNOWLEDGMENTS

With gratitude and appreciation, I acknowledge the collective consciousness of the wise souls who encouraged, supported, and contributed to the energy of this book.

To my enlightened team of spiritual guides, that inspired and channeled universal wisdom to me: Celestine (crown), White Eagle (third eye), Edgar (throat), Mary (heart), Lion Heart (solar plexus), Wei (sacral), and Michael (root).

To the intellectual teachers, who have encouraged the expansion of my consciousness through their teachings: Edgar Cayce, Carl Jung, Caroline Myss, Rudolph Steiner, Christ, and Buddha.

To my associates, who exemplified the emotional expression of this work: Michael Wiese and his publishing team at Divine Arts — Gary Sunshine (editor), Debbie Berne (designer), Ken Lee, and Travis Masch — for illuminating the message in the presentation of this book; Faith Nolton, for artistically enhancing the energetic meaning of this book with her gorgeous illustrations; and Kevin Bender, April Cole, and Judy Peterson for encouragement and support reviewing the manuscript.

To the many inspiring people whom I have had the fortunate experience to educate, coach, and counsel with spiritual readings and workshops, I appreciate your informative interactions about consciousness and the wisdom of the soul. You have all helped me better understand the magnificence of our energy being.

Printed in the United States
by Baker & Taylor Publisher Services